Three White Sheep

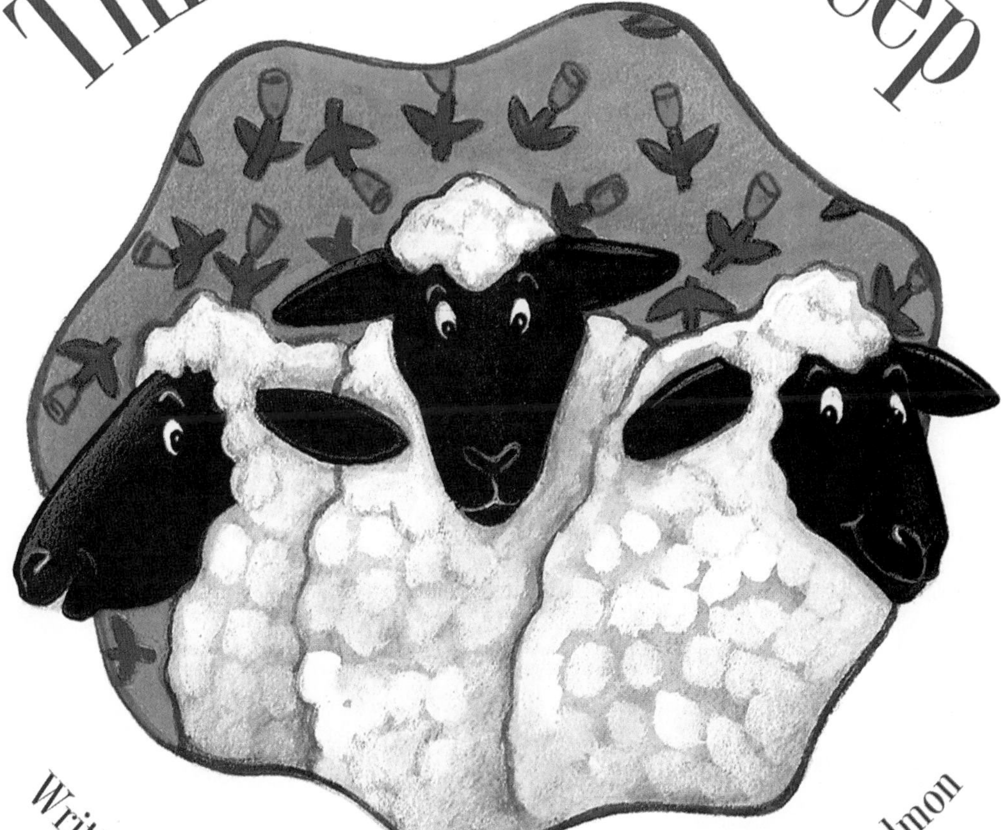

Written by Kathryn E. Lewis Illustrated by Deborah Melmon

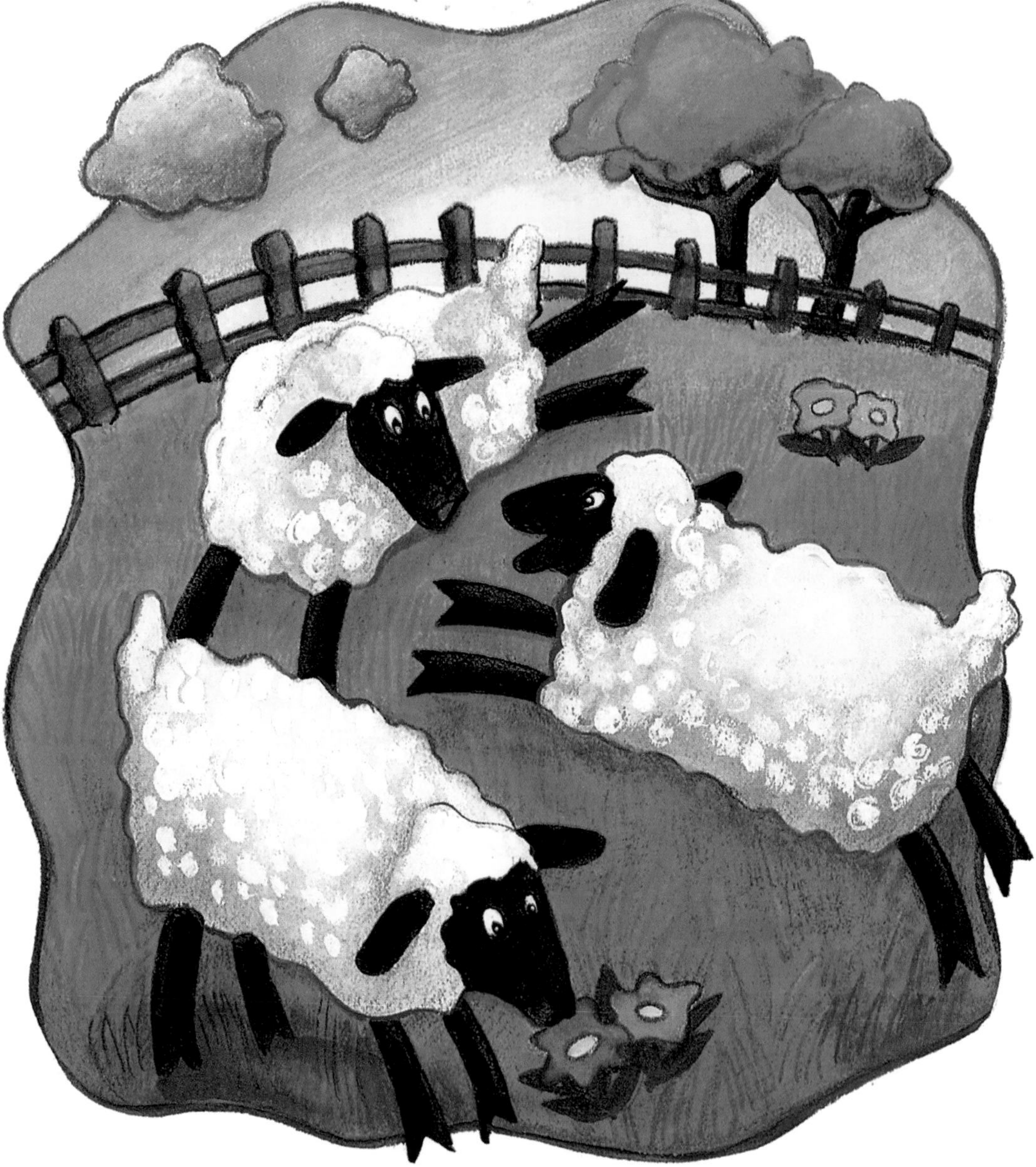

Three white sheep

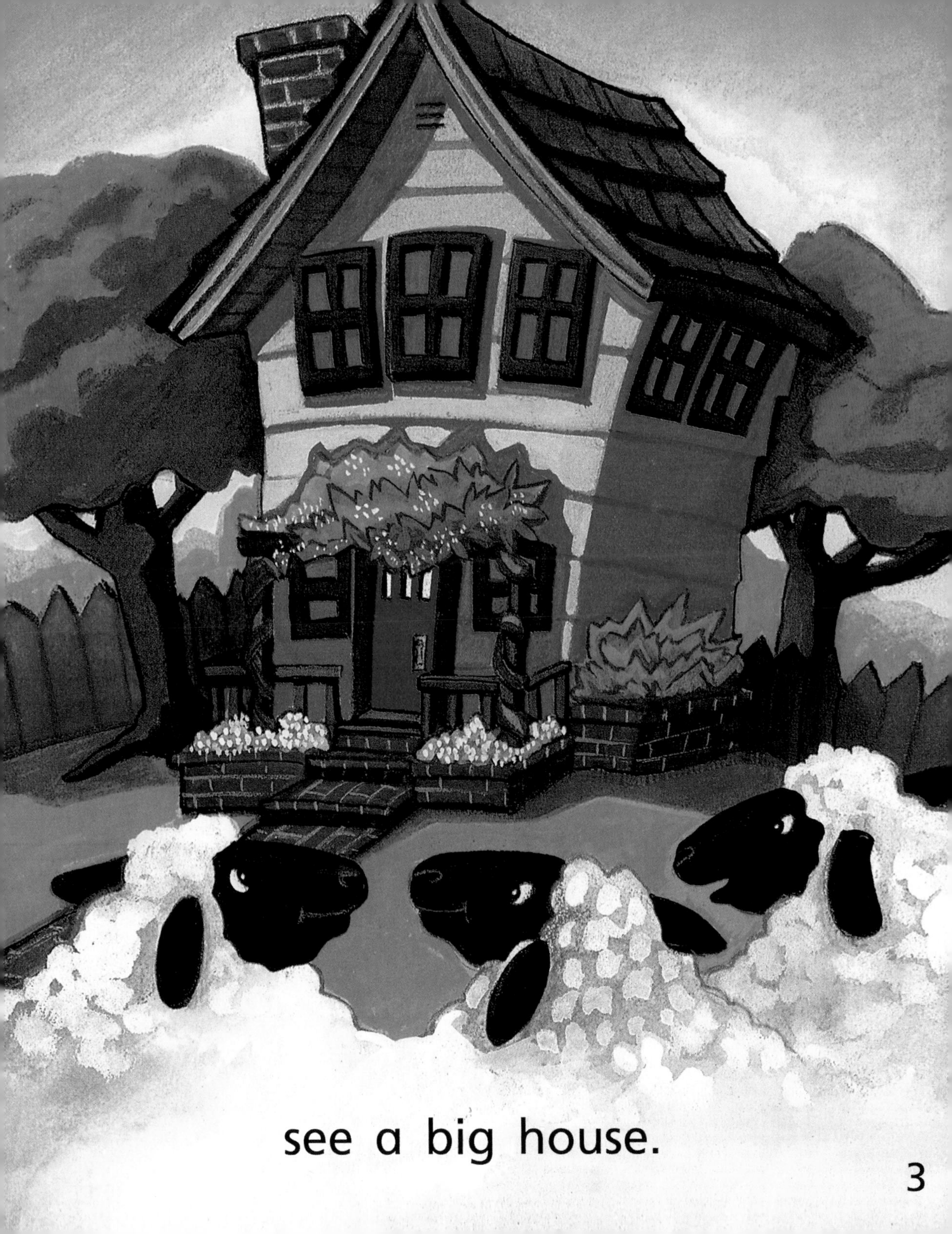

see a big house.

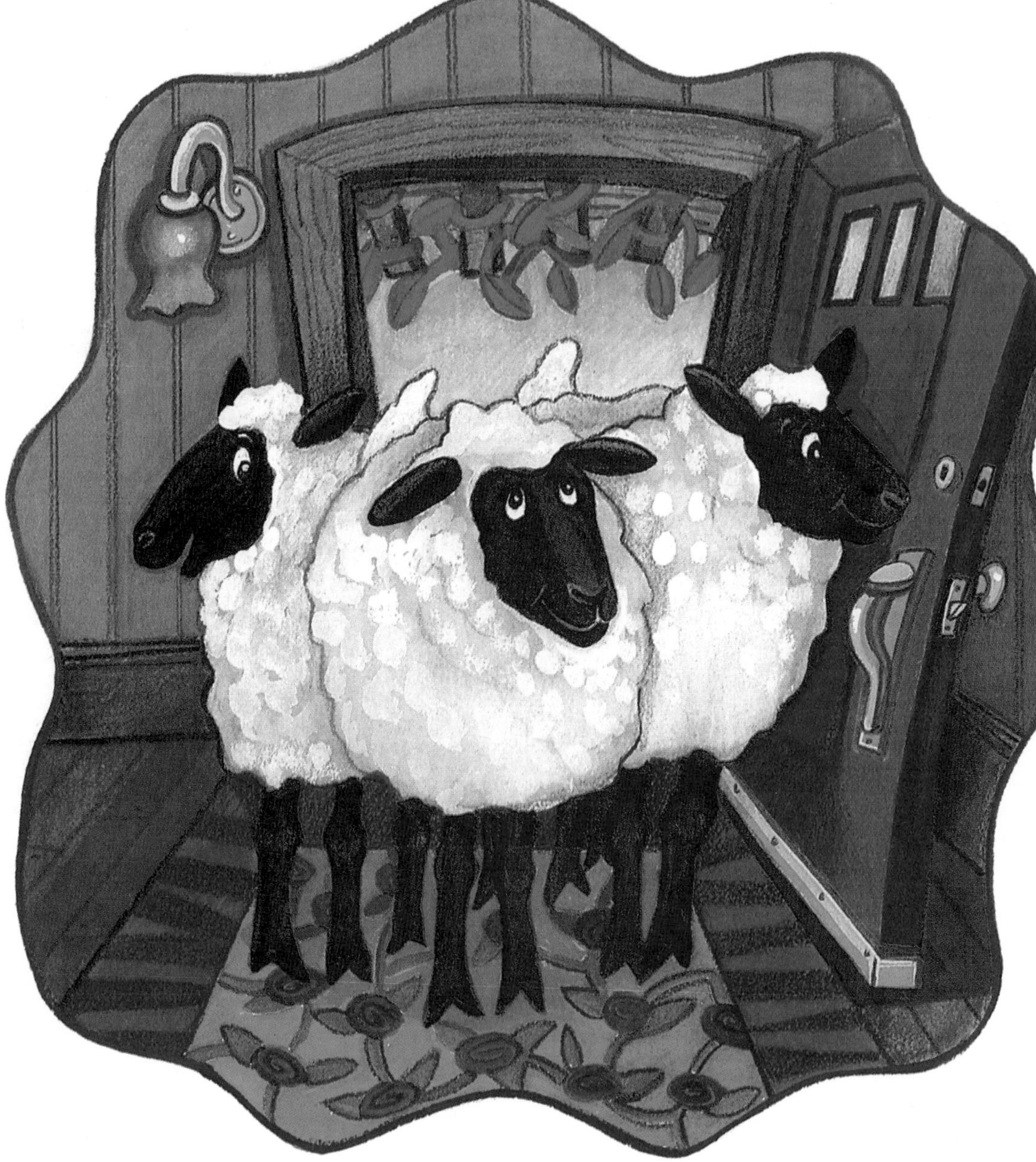

Three white sheep

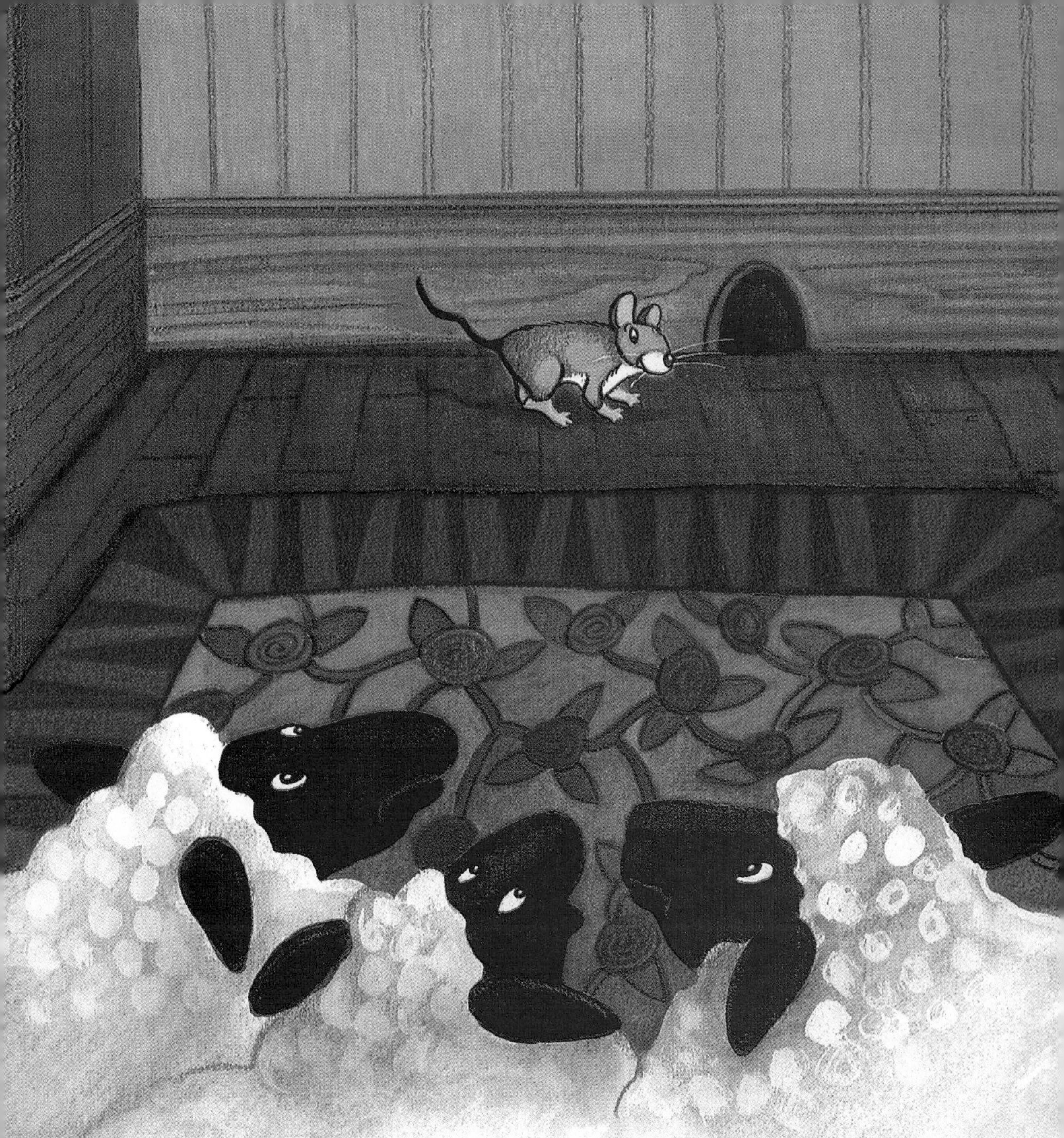

see a little mouse.

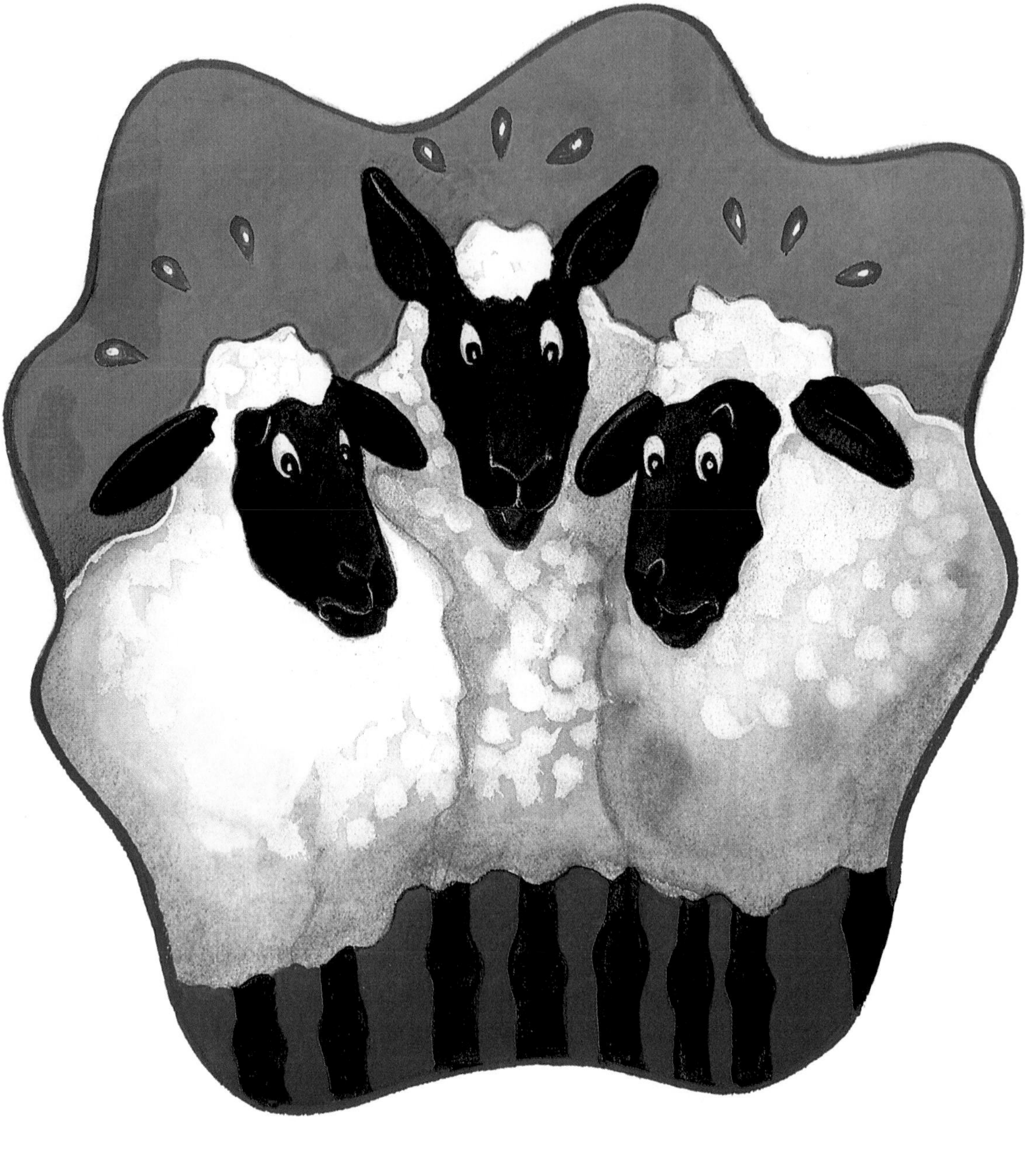

Three white sheep

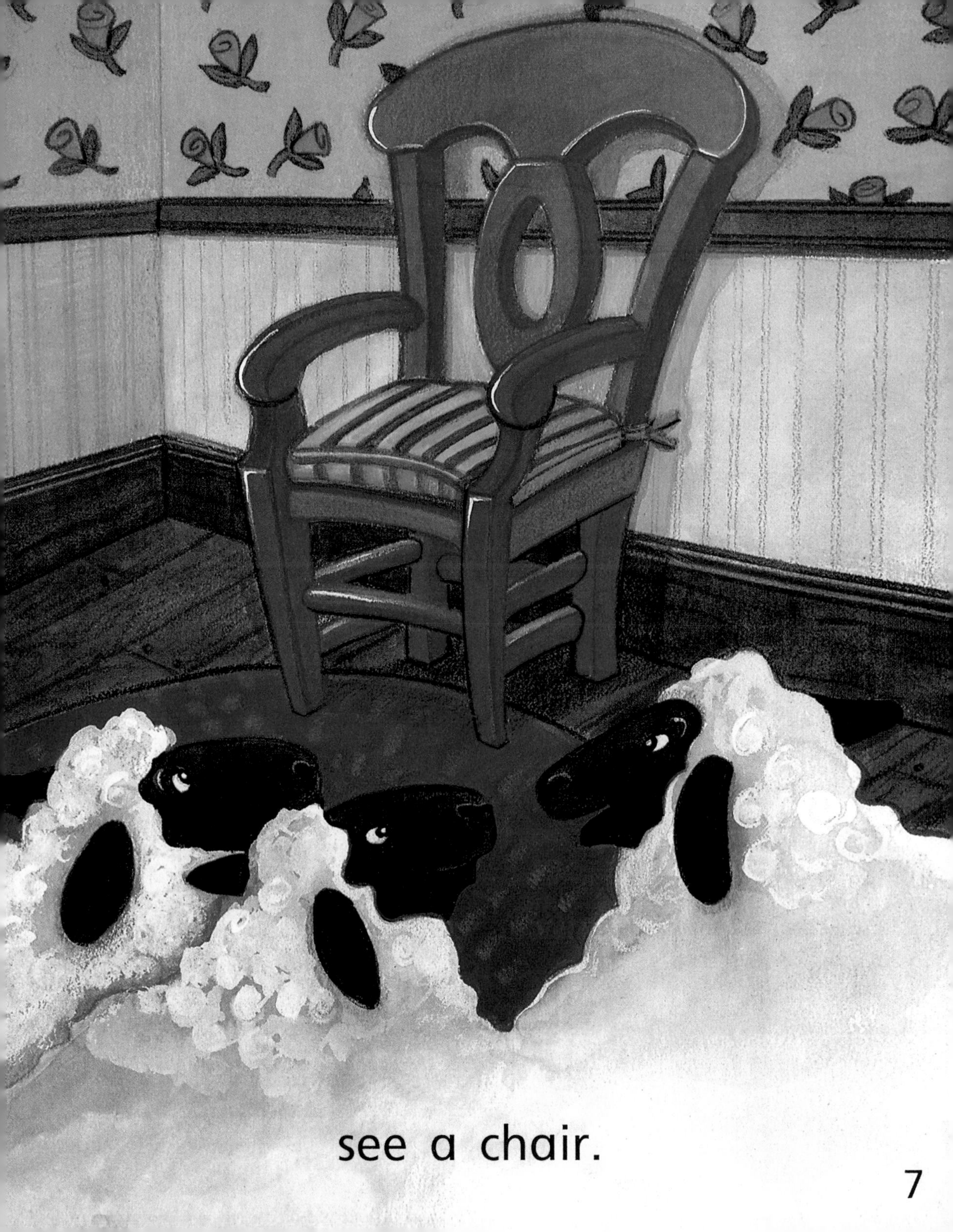

see a chair.

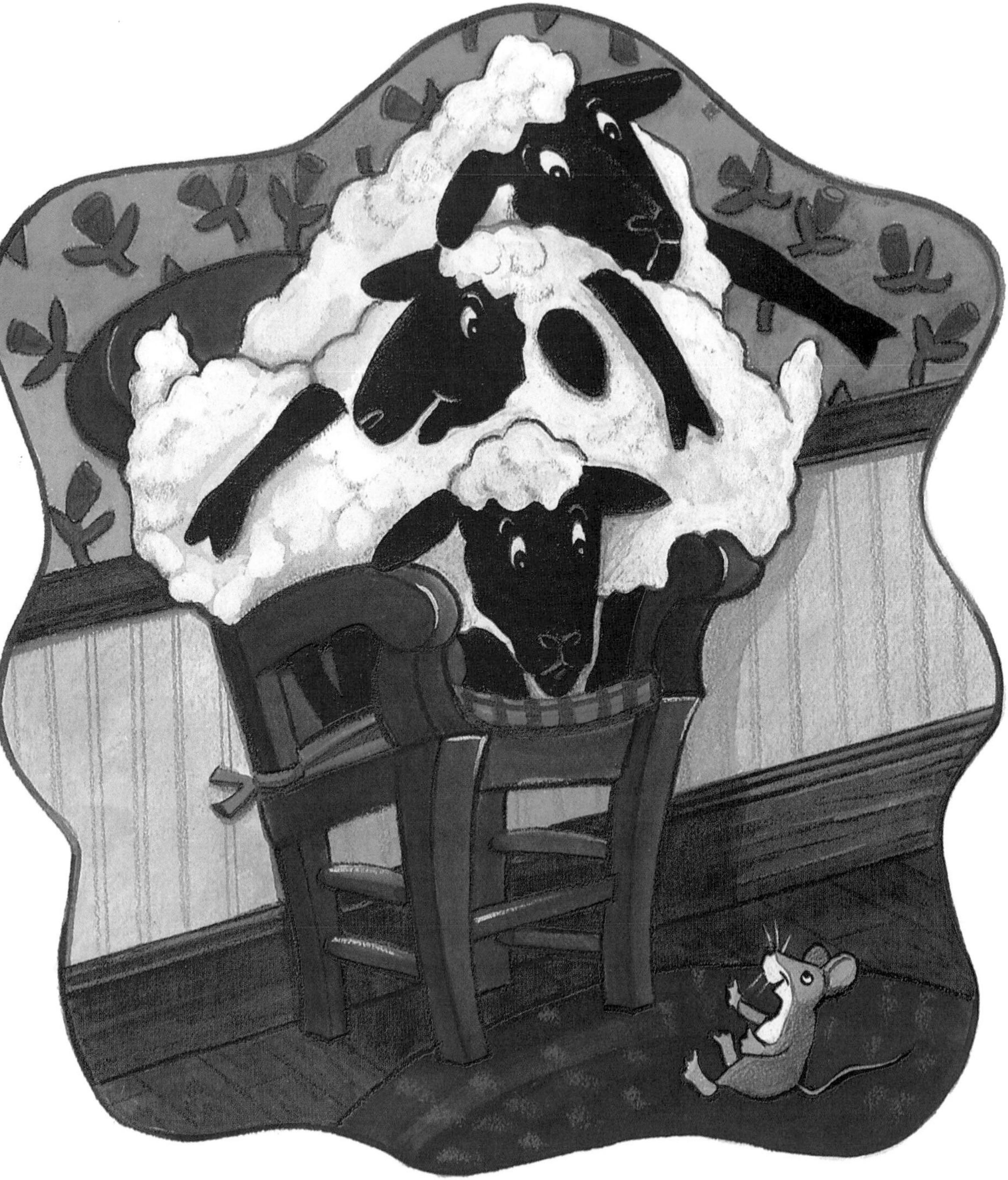